North American
INDIAN NATIONS
NATIVE PEOPLES
of the
SOUTHWEST

Linda Lowery

LERNER PUBLICATIONS ◆ MINNEAPOLIS

The editors would like to note that we have made every effort to work with consultants from various nations, as well as fact-checkers, to ensure that this content is accurate and appropriate. In addition to this title, we encourage readers to seek out content produced by the nations themselves online and in print.

Content Consultant: Alyce Sadongei, Project Coordinator for the American Indian Language Development Institute at the University of Arizona

Lerner Publications Company
A division of Lerner Publishing Group, Inc.
241 First Avenue North
Minneapolis, MN 55401 USA

For reading levels and more information, look up this title at www.lernerbooks.com.

Main body text set in Rockwell Std Light 12/16.
Typeface provided by Monotype Typography.

Library of Congress Cataloging-in-Publication Data

Lowery, Linda, 1949–
    Native peoples of the southwest / by Linda Lowery.
        pages cm. — (North American Indian nations)
    Audience: Grades 4–6.
    ISBN 978-1-4677-7936-4 (lb : alk. paper) — ISBN 978-1-4677-8329-3 (pb : alk. paper) — ISBN 978-1-4677-8330-9 (eb pdf)
        1. Indians of North America—Southwest, New—Juvenile literature. I. Title.
E78.S7L69 2015
979.004'97—dc23   2015001941

Manufactured in the United States of America
1 – PC – 7/15/16

CONTENTS

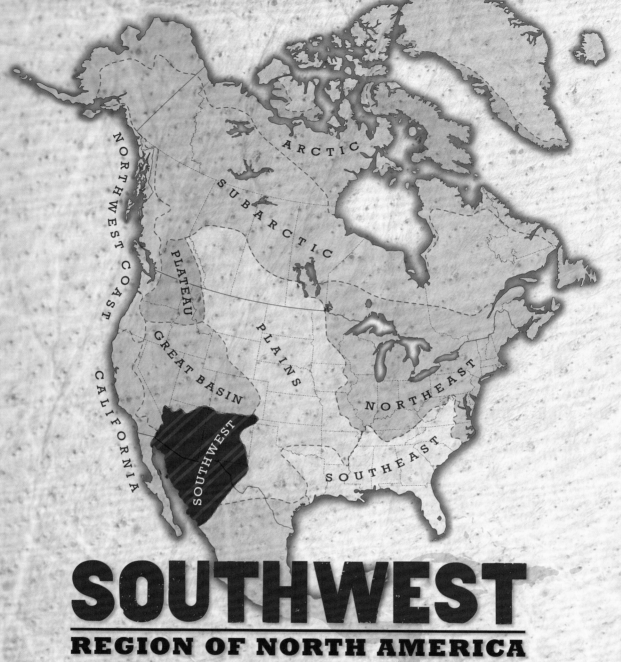

SOUTHWEST
REGION OF NORTH AMERICA

CULTURAL REGIONS OF THE UNITED STATES AND CANADA

- Plateau
- Northwest Coast
- California
- Plains
- Southeast
- Southwest
- Great Basin
- Northeast
- Subarctic
- Arctic
- Other

- – – – Cultural area border
- ──── International border
- ·········· State/province border

INTRODUCTION

Two of Sky Father's sons went down to the Fourth World, where the people lived. The Fourth World was dark and crowded. The brothers wanted to lead them to the sunny Fifth World up above. So the brothers built a ladder. The people climbed up through the Third, Second, and First Worlds. At last they reached the Fifth World, where they have lived ever since.

Zuni (ZOO-nee) people use this story to explain how they came to live in the American Southwest. It is just one of many ancient stories told by American Indians of this region.

These stories have probably been told since people started living in the region, at least twenty thousand years ago. Many Southwest Indians believe their ancestors always lived in North America. Some scientists believe that people originally came from Asia at least twenty thousand years ago. During the Ice Age, nomadic hunters walked across a land bridge and gradually spread out across North America.

Many different groups settled in the Southwest region of what eventually became the United States. These peoples made their homes in the mountains, deserts, plateaus, and canyons of the region. They developed ways of life based on the climate and landscape.

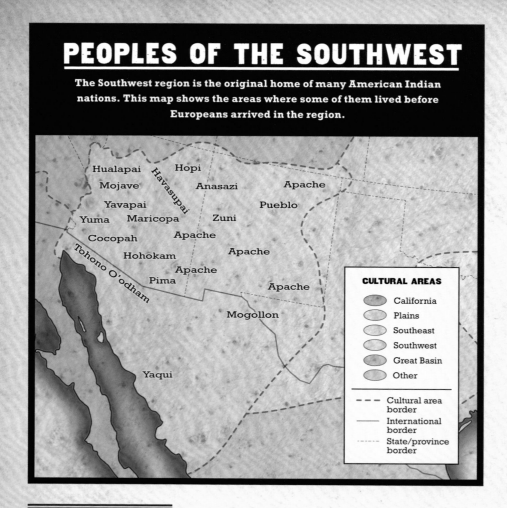

PEOPLES OF THE SOUTHWEST

The Southwest region is the original home of many American Indian nations. This map shows the areas where some of them lived before Europeans arrived in the region.

Hualapai
Hopi
Mojave
Havasupai
Anasazi
Apache
Yavapai
Pueblo
Yuma
Maricopa
Zuni
Cocopah
Apache
Hohokam
Apache
Tohono O'odham
Apache
Pima
Apache
Mogollon
Yaqui

CULTURAL AREAS

- California
- Plains
- Southeast
- Southwest
- Great Basin
- Other

- - - Cultural area border
—— International border
----- State/province border

Many Peoples

The earliest people to settle the Southwest were the Anasazi (ah-nuh-SAH-zee). They lived in Chaco Canyon in present-day Mexico. There, they built cliff dwellings with enough rooms for four thousand people. The settlement was the center of trade for ancient Southwest Indians until about 1000 CE. About 400 miles (644 kilometers) of dirt roads connected it to other villages in the region.

By 1300, the Anasazi moved from Chaco Canyon to other

parts of present-day New Mexico. Other peoples settled farther west. The Hohokam (ho-ho-KUM) lived in the southern part of present-day Arizona by the Gila and Salt Rivers. The Mogollon (moh-go-YONE) lived farther south in the desert mountains of modern-day Arizona, New Mexico, and Mexico.

These ancient groups eventually vanished. But their descendants spread throughout the Southwest. Many Pueblo (PWEB-lo) peoples settled along the Rio Grande, a river that runs through parts of present-day Texas, New Mexico, and Colorado. The Zuni lived farther west, in present-day New Mexico. The Hopi (HO-pee) lived near the Grand Canyon in modern-day Arizona.

The Pima (PEE-muh) and Tohono O'odham (toh-HO-no oh-OH-dum) lived far south, near present-day Mexico. The

This Anasazi construction in Chaco Canyon is named Kin Kletso, or "yellow house." It has sixty-five rooms. Archaeologists have dated it to around 1125 CE.

Peoples of the Southwest lived in a variety of landscapes. Most of those landscapes were dry, like the land in this photo taken in the Sonoran Desert of Arizona.

Navajo (NAH-vuh-ho) lived close to the Hopi and Zuni, near the Grand Canyon. The Apache (uh-PAH-chee) traveled through hot southern deserts, including land in present-day Texas, New Mexico, and Arizona.

Other peoples lived in the western part of present-day Arizona. The Yuma (YEW-muh) and Mojave (mo-HAH-vay) lived along the Colorado River. The Yavapai (YAH-vuh-pie) and Hualapai (WAH-lah-pie) had settled along the rim of the Grand Canyon. The Havasupai (ah-vah-SOO-pie) lived in the Grand Canyon itself, surrounded by red sandstone and sparkling waterfalls.

Southwest peoples spoke different languages from six main language families. Other languages, called isolates, were also spoken. Each language family included many different but related languages. A single language might also have several different versions, or dialects. But people still found ways to communicate even if they spoke different dialects or languages. One way was by using sign language.

Peoples that belonged to the same language group often shared many other cultural traits. But they did not always have the same government. For example, all Apache speak the same language and have a common culture. But this group is made up of six smaller, independent groups. Each subgroup has its

LANGUAGE FAMILIES OF SOUTHWEST PEOPLES

LANGUAGE FAMILY	CULTURAL GROUP
Tanoan (three subgroups: Tiwa, Tewa, and Towa)	Pueblo
Keresan	Pueblo
Zuni	Zuni
Uto-Aztecan	Hopi, Pima, Tohono O'odham, Yaqui (yah-KEE)
Athabaskan	Apache, Navajo
Hokan	Cocopah (kwee-KUH-puh), Havasupai, Hualapai, Maricopa (mayr-ee-KOH-puh), Mojave, Yavapai, Yuma

THE SAME PEOPLE, MANY NAMES

American Indian peoples have their own names for themselves and for neighboring peoples. When Europeans came to North America, they sometimes made up new names for American Indian nations. Or they used a name that another American Indian group had made up. For example, Anasazi is a Navajo name for the ancestors of many modern Southwest Indian peoples. The name means "ancient ones" or "ancient enemies." Most Southwest Indians do not use this name. They use names that mean "ancient ones" in their own languages. Many modern Southwest peoples are still known by several names. The name Navajo comes from a Tewa Pueblo word. The Navajo call themselves the Diné, which means "the people."

own leaders and traditions. The same is true for the Pueblo.

Members of different Southwestern groups frequently exchanged goods. They also traded with Plains Indians for buffalo robes. Southwest Indians traded with native peoples from present-day California and Mexico for shells and bird feathers.

Traditional and Modern

When Spanish explorers arrived in the 1600s, at least twenty thousand Southwest Indians were living in the area that later became Arizona, New Mexico, southwestern Colorado, and southeastern Utah. But native peoples lived in canyons, caves, and mountains. These areas were hard for Europeans to reach. So the population in the Southwest might have been far higher than Europeans guessed.

In the twenty-first century, Southwest Indian populations have grown. Southwest Indians are citizens of the United States. They are connected to the modern world. Yet they stay true to their traditional roots. Some modern Pueblo people live in adobe homes built into cliffs. Many Havasupai spend summers deep in the cool Grand Canyon and winters on the sunny plateau on the rim. People speak their native languages at home. Many Southwest Indians say that no matter how many centuries pass, they will remain deeply connected to their ancestors.

CHAPTER 1

A DESERT HOMELAND

The Southwest is a dramatic landscape of pine forests, deserts, mesas, and canyons. But it is dry, with little rainfall and very hot summers. For centuries, Southwest Indians lived according to the weather and the land. They were skilled at using their unique landscape and surroundings for shelter, food, and clothing.

Some peoples were nomadic, moving frequently from place to place. Others were seminomadic. They had different homes for winter and summer. For instance, in winter, the Havasupai lived on sunny, rugged plateaus in what became northwestern Arizona. In summer, they moved down into the Grand Canyon, which was cooler and had water to grow crops. Many groups moved in summer to escape the most intense heat and to be near precious water.

Shelter

Southwest Indians built homes that would work for their climates and lifestyles. Nomadic peoples, such as the Apache, built dome-shaped huts called wickiups. Wickiups could be put up and taken down easily, which helped communities move from place to place.

The seminomadic Navajo lived in the deserts and canyons of present-day northern New Mexico and Arizona. Their sturdy homes, called hogans, were round or octagonal. The frames were made of logs, earth, and rocks. A hole in the roof let smoke escape when they cooked over a fire inside. The entrance of a hogan faced east, toward the sunrise, which is sacred to the Navajo and many other Southwest peoples.

Some peoples had different homes for different times of the year. In the winter, the Havasupai built cone-shaped shelters out of sticks. They covered the walls with earth to keep out cold air. In the summer, they built oval-shaped huts from thatch and brush. Because of the warm weather, they used these huts only for sleeping.

An Apache wickiup dwelling in Arizona

The adobe homes in Taos Pueblo near the present-day city of Taos, New Mexico, were built between 1000 and 1450 CE. Taos Pueblo is one of the oldest, continuously inhabited American Indian communities in the United States.

Other peoples had permanent homes. The Eastern Pueblo lived in villages with adobe houses. Women built these homes from adobe brick. Several buildings might be attached. Others stood alone as single houses. The entrances to Pueblo homes faced south to get good sunlight throughout the day.

In the far south, many villages had ramadas. These wide-open structures had flat roofs held up by sturdy poles. There, people could gather in the cool shade. The Tohono O'odham, the Pima, and the Yaqui were among the southern groups that used ramadas.

Water

Southwest Indians worked hard to capture every drop of rare rain and snow. Women made tightly woven baskets of reeds

MOVEMENT OF SOUTHWEST PEOPLES

LIFESTYLE	CULTURAL GROUPS
Settled (living in one place)	Pueblo
Seminomadic	Pima, Navajo, Havasupai, Hualapai, Mojave, Tohono O'odham, Yaqui, Yavapai, Zuni
Nomadic	Pima, Apache, Yuma, Yavapai

and grass so they could carry water. Women also made pots of baked clay, which they filled with water. Their families could use this water for drinking, cooking, and watering crops.

The Pueblo often lived and farmed far from water. So they dug canal systems that carried water from rivers and streams to their crops. The Pueblo also built dams. The dams kept rainwater contained in one area, so that it would not wash away and evaporate.

This woven basket sealed with pine pitch (a sticky substance from the bark of pine trees) was used to store and carry water.

Other groups had even less access to water. The Hopi and Zuni lived on the Colorado Plateau in present-day Arizona. There were no rivers nearby. So they relied on small springs that trickled down the cliffs. The Hopi also practiced dry farming. They made holes in the desert, dropped seeds inside, and watered each seed with a small amount of melted snow or rainwater.

Food

Corn was the most important crop for Southwest Indians. Women ground up corn into flour, which they made into bread or tortillas. They also cooked corn as mush. Or they cooked the corn with other plants or mixed it with meat. The Hopi prepared corn in more than fifty ways. They grew red, blue, yellow, and white corn. Their specialty dish was piki, a thin blue corn bread.

This painting by W. Langdon Kihn (1898–1957) shows Laguna women making piki—a thin, rolled corn bread made from blue corn.

Most Southwest Indians also grew squash, pumpkins, and kidney beans. After Europeans came to the area, many groups began growing wheat.

Not all groups relied on farming. The Navajo mainly hunted and fished. Their Pueblo neighbors taught them to grow corn too.

The Apache got most of their food by hunting. Rabbits, deer, lizards, snakes, and small wild pigs provided food. The Pueblo sometimes ate small animals and birds, such as wild turkeys. The Havasupai and Hualapai hunted antelope and deer during winter months when they didn't farm.

This engraving by a European artist illustrates crops planted by the Zuni people in New Mexico.

Diets also included foods that grew naturally on the land. The Havasupai and Hualapai gathered pine nuts and berries. The Apache collected berries, wild chilies, mesquite beans, and cactus fruits. The Tohono O'odham used the fruit of the saguaro. This huge cactus was common in their territory. Its fruit could be made into jams and jellies.

CEREMONIAL CLOTHES

Southwest Indians customarily wore elaborate clothes for ceremonies. Many of them still do. People traditionally used roots, berries, and flowers to dye clothing bright colors. Masks were made from wood, leather, or clay. Depending on the purpose of the ceremony, Southwest Indians wore bird feathers, deer antlers, ribbons, turtle shells, or body paint. The Hopi and Yaqui made decorative sashes from the cocoons of giant silk moths.

A Hopi woman's sash. It was worn as a belt during ceremonies, dances, and other special occasions.

Clothing

Pueblo women wore simple wrapped dresses made from the cotton they grew. They often dyed the fabric blue using sunflower seeds. Most Pueblo men wore breechcloths—pieces of animal hide wrapped between their legs and tied around the waist. Others wore kilts, which were similar to skirts, made of animal skins. In cold weather, they added leggings. Moccasins protected people's feet in all seasons.

The Apache and Navajo made most of their clothing from deerskin. In later years, the Pueblo taught the Navajo how to use cotton. Cotton was much cooler than animal skin, so it worked well for hot environments. The Navajo learned to weave blankets and ponchos that kept them warm in snowy winters. Apache and Navajo women and men wore turquoise and shell jewelry, often set in copper. The Mojave decorated their clothing with geometric designs.

Later, when the Spanish came to the region, Southwest Indians borrowed clothing ideas from them. Jewelry makers began to use silver instead of copper. Navajo women began wearing big gathered skirts of brightly dyed cotton. Apache men wore military jackets and tied cotton scarves around their heads.

A young Hopi woman dresses in a woven-cotton garment and belt bearing traditional designs. She also wears turquoise jewelry made from the beautiful blue rock found in many places in the Southwest.

CHAPTER 2

COMMUNITY AND
SPIRITUALITY

Family and community were very important to **Southwest Indians.** Sometimes parents, children, grandparents, and cousins shared a home. The Zuni lived this way, for instance. Among some nations, including the Navajo, only parents and children lived in the same dwelling. A village was made up of groups of extended families. Several villages in the same area might form a larger group called a band.

Southwest Indians also belonged to clans. Everyone in a clan was related, and members were loyal to one another. Members of several different clans might live in the same village. Different clans were responsible for hosting certain ceremonies and for keeping certain sacred objects.

In most Southwest cultures, clan membership was passed down through women. When two people married, a man became part of his wife's clan. Children belonged to their mother's clan. But in some Tanoan-speaking Pueblo cultures, clans were passed down through men. Usually, a person could not marry someone from the same clan. Among the Pima, though, members of the same clan could marry each other.

Roles and Leadership

Men and women were given equal respect in Southwest cultures. They had different responsibilities, though. Women were in charge of the family. They built and owned houses. They also made clothing, tended crops, and prepared food.

Men hunted and held councils. At councils, men performed sacred rituals and discussed important decisions. Some men were also chiefs.

Villages and bands often had one or more chiefs to make military and spiritual decisions. The Pima had one main chief who was in charge of councils. Each Pima village also had its own chief who handled farming and defense. A Pueblo village might have one chief who was a spiritual leader and served for life. Every year, that chief chose two other war chiefs who handled military matters. Chiefs could be chosen in many different ways. For instance, the chief of a Havasupai band usually inherited his role. In other groups, such as Apache villages, council members elected a chief.

CEREMONIAL PIPES

Ceremonial pipes were very important to many Southwest peoples. The Pueblo made clay pipes called cloud blowers. Medicine men smoked from them and then blew the smoke toward each of the four directions: east, west, north, and south. This connected them to the spirit world. Medicine men passed pipes around while praying for help with important decisions.

Healers, sometimes called medicine men and medicine women, were honored spiritual leaders. These men and women healed the sick and led ceremonies. Navajo healers were called singers. They performed ceremonies called chantways and Blessing Ways. These traditions helped Southwest Indians stay in harmony with the universe through births, deaths, and other important events. Medicine men and women could also be military leaders.

Spirituality

To the peoples of the Southwest, everything in nature was sacred. They believed all things had a spirit: animals, birds, trees, rocks, lightning, rain, and wind. Each culture had a creation story. These stories often featured spiders, lizards, snakes, and other animals that taught humans how to live well.

This image shows the inside of a Pueblo kiva.

Most Southwest Indians believed their people emerged from beneath the ground through an opening. The Apache believe they left the underworld by crawling up a cane stalk. Pueblo peoples have a similar story. They call the opening a sipapu.

Pueblo villages had kivas, underground chambers for

Kachina dolls represent a variety of supernatural forms.

sacred ceremonies and meetings. The kivas had a small hole in the bottom to represent the sacred sipapu. Each kiva had a religious society connected to it. A man might belong to several religious societies.

Kachinas were supernatural beings who carried messages between the spirits and the Pueblo. Kachinas lived in the underworld and came out through a sipapu to visit for half the year. The Hopi and Zuni believed in more than one hundred different kachinas.

Gatherings and Dances

Most Southwest peoples held big gatherings a few times a year. All the communities of a nation came together for these events. People might gather for corn shucking or for an important ceremonial rain dance.

SACRED BEINGS OF SOUTHWEST PEOPLES

CULTURAL GROUP	MAJOR SACRED BEINGS
Navajo	The Holy People (including Earth Mother, First Man, and First Woman)
Hopi	Kachinas (including White Bear, Squash, and Butterfly Maiden)
Apache	Usen (or Ussen), the giver of life
Pima, Tohono O'odham	Jeweḍ Ma:kai
Mojave	Mastamho, Great Spirit's younger brother, who created the Colorado River

When the Tohono O'odham or the Pueblo met for a group deer hunt, everyone first danced a deer dance. This dance blessed both the hunters and the animals they would hunt. Most hunts included only men and boys. Hopi communities met for rabbit hunts. Afterward, the whole group danced and celebrated.

Other gatherings marked important moments in people's lives. When a Navajo or Apache girl was about fifteen, nation members danced in her honor. If she was Apache, she wore an

A Zuni jar *(left)* and two Acoma jars. Like the Zuni, the Acoma lived outside of present-day Albuquerque, New Mexico.

many colors. When the Hopi painted designs on pottery, they used paintbrushes made from yucca leaves. They still do this.

Symbols and Colors

Southwest Indians used many symbols in their art. Special colors, stones, and animals represented the four directions. For the Navajo, the colors of north, south, east, and west were black, blue, white, and yellow. For the Hualapai, yellow, black, white, and red stood for the colors of the Grand Canyon.

The Zuni painted six animals on their pottery. These animals were the mountain lion, badger, wolf, bear, eagle, and mole. The first four animals each stood for one of the four directions. The Zuni also believed that "above" and "below" were directions. The eagle was the symbol for above, and the mole was the symbol for below.

Specialty Crafts

Different Southwest cultures specialized in various crafts. The Navajo were skilled weavers. Legend says that they learned

AL QOYAWAYMA

Al Qoyawayma makes a living as an engineer and educator. But this multitalented member of the Hopi community is also a skilled potter and sculptor. He uses Arizona clay and traditional Hopi pottery-making techniques. "It's like having a time machine," he says of his art. "You've sampled something . . . of the past by working with the same materials and the same methods." But he also explores new ideas. For instance, he experiments with different shades of mineral paints when he decorates his pots, vases, and sculptures. Blending the shades creates a "rainbow effect" that sets his work apart from ancient Hopi art.

how to weave from Spider Woman. Weaving changed after the Spanish brought sheep to the Southwest in the early 1500s. The Navajo began to raise sheep and use wool instead of cotton. Navajo rugs are still made by hand from wool and can take months to finish.

The Apache, Hopi, and Navajo made beautiful jewelry from turquoise. After the Spanish brought silver to North America, nations started making jewelry with silver as well. The Hopi's silver jewelry had two layers. The top layer had cutout designs on it. Beneath these designs, the blackened lower layer was visible.

The Hopi and Zuni made colorfully painted kachina masks and dolls with clay, feathers, and wood. Each kachina represented a part of nature, such as plants, insects, water, rain, sun, and animals. Every Hopi girl had a kachina doll and learned about the spirits by playing with her doll.

For the Cochiti Pueblo, the most important craft was the

drum. People made drums from dead, hollow aspen tree trunks that they covered with leather. Drums, rattles, and whistles made sounds to represent animal hooves, birds, rainfall, and the beating of the heart.

Arts in the Modern Southwest

In modern times, many museums display Southwest Indian arts and crafts. For instance, the Heard Museum in Phoenix, Arizona, includes collections of Hopi kachina dolls, Zuni jewelry, and Navajo cloth. Many Soutwest nations have their own museums and arts centers too. The Pima run the Huhugam Heritage Center just outside of Phoenix. It features beautiful displays of basketry and pottery. In addition, some artists from Southwest Indian cultures create modern forms of art, such as digitally created pieces, and put them on display.

A Navajo Yeibeichai rug with female dancers

CHAPTER 4

CONTACT WITH
EUROPEANS

The first European explorers came to the Southwest from Spain in the sixteenth century. They had heard a legend about seven cities made of gold. In 1540, Francisco Coronado and his men arrived in the Zuni village of Hawikuh. The explorers discovered that the settlements were not made of gold. Spanish soldiers treated the Zunis badly. The Zuni resisted. They chased the Spanish back to Mexico.

In 1598, Juan de Oñate arrived in the region with missionaries and other men. This time, the Spanish did not want gold. They wanted land. Oñate set up a government at the Ohkay Owingeh Pueblo village in present-day New Mexico. The first church in the Southwest was built there. Catholic priests outlawed native religions. To keep the peace, American Indians went to church on Sundays. In secret, they continued their own spiritual practices.

By the mid-1600s, the Spanish had spread all across the Southwest. They used American Indians as slaves to build homes, grind corn, and find water. Many native peoples died from diseases carried by Europeans.

Revolts and Treaties

Southwest Indians grew tired of abuse. In 1680, the Pueblo and Apache peoples joined together under the leadership of Popé, a Tewa Pueblo man. Popé led a large group of warriors in the Pueblo-Apache Revolt. Cliff dwellings were perfect fortresses. The Pueblo Indians pulled up their ladders to keep the Spanish out. Using only stones and arrows, the warriors held back the Europeans for two years. This revolt was the most successful American Indian resistance to Europeans anywhere in North America.

But throughout the eighteenth century, miners, Catholic priests, soldiers, and other Europeans kept arriving. They wanted American Indians to move off the land so they could build communities. Many Southwest nations signed treaties with

Visitors to Mesa Verde National Park in Colorado can tour Cliff Palace, original cliff dwellings of the Pueblo Indians. These homes, built into high cliffs, helped the Pueblo and Apache protect themselves while they held off European invaders.

New Spain. These treaties said Europeans would be allowed to use certain parts of native land. The rest of the land would be off-limits to the Europeans. But the Spanish did not honor the treaties. Instead, the newcomers and the government used the area's natural resources freely, as if they owned all the American Indian land.

The Pima attacked people who had invaded their land. Battles broke out between the Pima and Spanish forces. White newcomers called this the Pima Revolt (1751–1752). After four months of fighting, the Pima surrendered.

Fighting for Homelands

In 1854, the United States bought present-day Arizona and New Mexico from Mexico. The US government wanted to relocate Southwest Indians to make way for incoming railroads, mining, and new settlements. Government leaders decided to move American Indians to small areas of land called reservations.

Southwest Indians fought to keep control of their homelands. The Navajo defended their lands in New Mexico and Arizona in many battles between 1849 and 1863. The Apache raided forts and Europeans' homes to try to drive the invading newcomers away.

But many native peoples were killed in battles. Entire families had died of sickness. One by one, most nations surrendered to the United States. The US Army moved the Zuni, Mojave, Pima, Maricopa, and other nations onto reservations.

The remaining Apache fought on. In 1871, however, Europeans at Camp Grant in present-day Arizona killed more than one hundred Apache people, mostly women and children. The Apache warriors surrendered. The US government moved Apache far from their homelands, to Alabama and Florida. But

GERONIMO AND HIS HOMELAND

The Apache leader Geronimo fought against forced moves to reservations until 1886. As an old man, Geronimo told the story of his life to a white man named S. M. Barrett. Barrett wrote down Geronimo's words, including these thoughts about the Apache people's strong ties to their lands:

> When [Apache sacred being] Usen created the Apaches, he also created their homes in the West. He gave to them such grain, fruits, and game as they needed to eat. To restore their health when disease attacked them He made many different herbs to grow. He taught them where to find these herbs, and how to prepare them for medicine. He gave the Apaches a pleasant climate and all they needed for clothing and shelter was at hand. . . . When they are taken from these homes they sicken and die. How long will it be until it is said [that] there are no Apaches?

one of their chiefs, Geronimo, refused to move to a reservation. He and twenty-four others escaped. Years later, they were finally caught. Geronimo was sent to Florida and imprisoned there in 1886.

Some nations succeeded in keeping portions of their land. In 1868, the US government decided the Navajo should move to a remote area in Oklahoma. They would be away from the rush of newcomers. The head Navajo chief was a medicine man named Barboncito. He talked with US leaders. Because of his efforts, the United States signed a treaty that allowed the Navajo to go back to their Arizona homeland. They have lived there ever since.

In this photo taken in 1900, American Indian students wearing European-style clothing draw a portrait during art class at Phoenix Indian School in Phoenix, Arizona.

More Changes

In the late nineteenth century, US government officials pressured American Indian parents to send their children to boarding schools run by missionaries. There, children were forbidden to speak their native languages. They were forced to leave behind their native ways.

But around the same time, some US policies toward American Indians began to change. In 1924, the Indian Citizenship Act allowed American Indians to become US citizens. The Indian Reorganization Act of 1934 allowed American Indian nations to set up their own governments on reservations.

Throughout the twentieth century, Southwest Indians pushed the US government to return native lands. Eventually, some groups found success. For instance, the Havasupai had lost much of their homeland near the Grand Canyon in 1919, when the area became a national park. The Havasupai had been forced to leave their winter homes on the plateau. The US government wanted them to stay down in the canyon year-round so tourists could visit the canyon rim. Deep in the canyon, the Havasupai had faced winters of heavy snow and only five hours of sunlight. But in 1975, the US government agreed to return some land to the Havasupai. Since then, the Havasupai have followed their tradition of living on the sunny plateau in winter and moving to the deep, cool canyon in summer.

Many other nations have worked to regain their lands and to protect the lands they still control. And despite the challenges they have faced for centuries, many have kept up their traditions as well.

NAVAJO CODE TALKERS

During World War II (1939–1945), the US military could not send radio messages because their Japanese enemies deciphered every code. Navajo marines developed a secret code using their native language. The Japanese were never able to break the code. During the war, 421 Navajo code talkers sent messages back and forth. Their messages saved many American lives during the war.

A two-man team of Navajo code talkers relay orders over a field radio during World War II.

CHAPTER 5

MIXING OLD AND NEW

Many Southwest American Indians say they live in **two different worlds.** One is the modern world. The other is their traditional world. Despite centuries of battles, slavery, and bans on their spiritual practices, the Southwest people have survived. In fact, most nations are growing and thriving.

Most Southwest Indians still live in Arizona, New Mexico, Utah, and Colorado. They do not live exactly the way they did hundreds of years ago. They use modern technology and conveniences. Still, nations try to remain true to their ancient ways. For special celebrations, children and adults dress in traditional cotton and deerskin clothing. They wear masks and headdresses and dance to honor the spirits. They practice their traditional religious customs as well.

Each Southwest nation is like a small country. Most Southwest Indian peoples live and work in other cities, but the reservations are their nation's centers. Southwest Indians return to reservations for holidays with their families. They come back to vote for council members who stay on the reservation to handle the nation's government. For instance, the council might decide whether to sell coal that is mined on their land. Or they might plan the details of an important feast day for the nation.

Earning a Living

Southwest Indians often go to cities to find jobs. Many people work in laboratories in Los Alamos and Santa Fe, New Mexico. In a few nations, such as the Zuni, many people make their living by selling silver and turquoise jewelry, kachina dolls, rugs, baskets, and pottery. About 90 percent of Zuni Nation members are able to live off the income from this work. The Hopi paint kachina dolls with natural colors made from ashes, clay, and ground stones. A finely crafted kachina doll can sell for thousands of dollars.

A Navajo artisan weaves a rug on a traditional loom.

Mules take visitors down steep trails to the bottom of the Grand Canyon in Arizona. Havasupai and Hualapai guides can earn a living taking park visitors through the canyon.

The Havasupai call themselves the guardians of the Grand Canyon. They earn money from tourism. They provide guides and mules for visitors to the canyon's South Rim. The Hualapai run tourist programs on their reservation at the canyon's West Rim.

The Navajo Nation sells the oil and coal deposits found on their land. The Apache run a ski resort at Sierra Blanca, a mountain in southern New Mexico. The Havasupai and Hualapai raise cattle. The money from these businesses mostly goes to the nation's government.

American Indians of the Southwest tend to be private. The Hopi, for instance, do not allow anyone to take photographs of their ceremonies or villages. Visitors must honor the ancient history of the area.

Keeping Traditions Alive

Southwest Indians work to preserve their native languages. The Hopi have written a dictionary of more than thirty thousand words. This helps children learn the language and participate in ceremonies. Several radio stations keep native languages alive as well. Arizona's KTNN-AM radio station airs programs in Navajo, Hopi, Apache, and Pueblo languages.

Southwest Indians pass on other traditions too. They teach their children ancient dances, songs, and prayers. Many say the old ways bring meaning to their lives and keep them connected to what is truly important.

The native peoples of the Southwest lived in a land with little rainfall and developed practical ways to work with nature. They survived droughts and floods, heavy winter snowfalls, and extremely hot summers. They fought to keep their homelands when newcomers claimed land that American Indians called home. They kept their spiritual beliefs even when the US government tried to prevent them from practicing ancient ways. In the twenty-first century, Southwest nations are thriving as they connect their ancient traditions and the modern world.

NOTABLE SOUTHWEST INDIAN PEOPLE

Annie Antone (Tohono O'odham)
is a basket weaver. She uses traditional methods and plant materials to make coiled baskets. Her baskets are famous for their detailed designs, which are partly inspired by ancient Southwest Indian pottery.

Notah Begay III (Navajo, San Felipe Pueblo, and Pueblo of Isleta)
is a professional golf player from New Mexico. He has won the PGA Tour tournament four times. He created a charity that aims to promote the health of American Indian youth.

Diane Humetewa (Hopi)
is a judge in charge of Arizona's highest court. In 2014, she became the first American Indian woman to serve as a federal judge. She decides important legal cases in the state and is an expert on laws related to American Indian nations.

R. Carlos Nakai (Navajo-Ute)
is a flute player. He writes and plays music inspired by the sounds of birds, water, and winds in the desert canyons where he lives.

Joanelle Romero (Apache)
is a filmmaker, actor, and music producer. She produces documentaries and other films about American Indian experiences. She has also started several American Indian film festivals and an American Indian-themed TV channel.

Luci Tapahonso (Navajo)
is an award-winning poet. She began writing poetry when she was around eight years old. She writes in the Navajo language, and many of her poems are about her nation's heritage.

Timeline

Each Southwest Indian culture had its own way of recording history. This timeline is based on the Gregorian calendar, which Europeans brought to North America.

1540 Francisco Coronado arrives on Zuni land.

1598 Juan de Oñate claims New Mexico as a Spanish colony in the New World.

1680 The Pueblo and Apache drive the Spanish from New Mexico in the Pueblo-Apache Revolt.

1700s New Spain signs treaties with many Southwest Indian nations.

1751 The Pima revolt against the Spanish.

1854 The United States gains areas of present-day Arizona and New Mexico.

1871 The US Army kills many unarmed Apache people at Camp Grant, and Apache people are sent to reservations.

1886 Geronimo is captured and imprisoned in Florida.

1924 The Indian Citizenship Act officially makes all American Indians US citizens.

1934 The Indian Reorganization Act recognizes independent governments of Plains American Indian nations.

1942–1945 Navajo servicemen become code talkers and play an important role in World War II.

1975 The Grand Canyon National Park Enlargement Act allows the Havasupai to return to their homeland near the Grand Canyon.

2015 The first World Indigenous Games took place in Palmas, Brazil. More than eighteen hundred indigenous people from twenty-three countries participated in the games, including many Southwest native peoples.

Glossary

adobe: a clay and sand mixture made into bricks or applied like plaster

agave: a plant that grows in the Southwest

council: a meeting to discuss important decisions and share advice

dialect: a form of one language that is spoken in different areas and may include unique words and pronunciations

language family: a group of related languages spoken by several nations

mesa: an elevated land with a flat top and sides with steep cliffs

nation: an independent group of people with a shared history, culture, and governing system

nomadic: traveling from place to place rather than settling in one spot

peoples: nations or groups of related nations

plateau: an area of level ground that is higher than the surrounding area

ramada: a wide-open structure that has a flat roof and is held up by sturdy poles

reservation: an area of land set aside for American Indians

ritual: an act that is performed in the same way each time, often as part of a religious or social ceremony

sacred: spiritually important and deserving of respect

saguaro: a large cactus that grows mostly in southern Arizona

seminomadic: living in at least two different areas based on the season

treaty: a formal written agreement by two or more parties

Source Notes

30 "Arizona Artforms: Al Qoyawayma," PBS video, 3:36, January 2, 2011, http://video.pbs.org/video/1718835986/.

35 Geronimo, *My Life: The Autobiography of Geronimo* (Tuscon, AZ: Fireship Press, 2009), 20–21.

Selected Bibliography

Fagan, Brian. *The First North Americans: An Archaeological Journey*. New York: Thames & Hudson, 2011.

Hirschfelder, Arlene, and Martha Kreipe de Montaño. *The Native American Almanac: A Portrait of Native America Today*. New York: Prentice Hall General Reference, 1993.

Jennings, Francis. *The Founders of America*. New York: Norton, 1993.

Minor, Marz, and Nono Minor. *The American Indian Craft Book*. Lincoln: University of Nebraska Press, 1978.

Treuer, Anton, et. al. *Indian Nations of North America*. Washington, DC: National Geographic, 2010.

LERNER

SOURCE

Expand learning beyond the printed book. Download free, complementary educational resources for this book from our website, www.lerneresource.com.

Further Information

Cunningham, Kevin, and Peter Benoit. *The Navajo*. New York: Children's Press, 2011. Learn more about the Navajo, including the code talkers, who helped the United States win World War II.

———. *The Pueblo*. New York: Children's Press, 2011. Learn more about the cliff dwellers.

Gimpel, Diane Marczely. *A Timeline History of Early American Indian Peoples*. Minneapolis: Lerner Publications, 2015. Explore more about the history of the Southwest Indians.

The Hopi Tribe
http://www.hopi-nsn.gov
Visit this official site of the Hopi to read the *Hopi Tutuveni* newspaper, learn about the tribal government, and learn more about Hopi history.

Indian Pueblo Cultural Center: Language
http://www.indianpueblo.org/19pueblos/language.html
Want to listen to the languages of the Pueblo? Go to this site where the Keresan, Tewa, Tiwa, Towa, and Zuni languages are spoken.

Pueblo Indian History for Kids
http://www.crowcanyon.org/EducationProducts/pueblo_history_kids
/introduction.asp
This website has a timeline where you can learn more about Pueblo history.

The Tohono O'odham Nation
http://www.tonation-nsn.gov
Explore this Tohono O'odham site to find fascinating information on history and culture, press releases related to the Tohono O'odham community, and more.

Index

Photo Acknowledgments

The images in this book are used with the permission of: © iStockphoto.com/Bastar (paper background); © lienkie/123RF.com (tanned hide background); © iStockphoto.com/FernandoAH, pp. 2–3; © Laura Westlund/Independent Picture Service, pp. 4, 6; © Scott S. Warren/National Geographic/Getty Images, p. 7; © iStockphoto.com/tonda, p. ≈8; © Marilyn Angel Wynn/Nativestock.com, pp. 13, 15, 18, 22; © Denkou Images/Alamy, p. 14; © National Geographic Image Collection/Alamy, p. 16; © North Wind Picture Archives/Alamy, p. 17; © Christie's Images/Corbis, pp. 23, 29; © Danny Lehman/Corbis, p. 27; © nik wheeler/Alamy, p. 31; © Corbis, pp. 32, 36; © Helena Lovincic/E+/Getty Images, p. 33; © Steven Allan/E+/Getty Images, p. 39; © Jose More/VWPics/Alamy, p. 40.

Front cover: © iStockphoto.com/Dean_Fikar.